IMAGES
of England

SKIPTON

A group of First World War soldiers of the Royal Garrison Artillery. Skiptonian Harry L. Thornton is pictured top right.

IMAGES
of England

SKIPTON

Compiled by
Ken Ellwood

TEMPUS

First published 1999
Copyright © Ken Ellwood, 1999

Tempus Publishing Limited
The Mill, Brimscombe Port,
Stroud, Gloucestershire, GL5 2QG

ISBN 0 7524 1612 X

Typesetting and origination by
Tempus Publishing Limited
Printed in Great Britain by
Midway Clark Printing, Wiltshire

This book is dedicated to my wife and family. Kathleen and I were married in the Church of Holy Trinity and although we are 'offcumdens' our children are Bradley and Skipton born and bred.

The Central Buildings are seen through Ship Corner arch, commemorating the Coronation of King George V in 1911.

Contents

High Street is a hive of activity, *c.* 1900. The hustle and bustle is of a very different character to that we are accustomed to today. Midland Bank, seen to the top right, was erected in 1888; next door is the Wheatsheaf Inn, which closed its doors in 1908.

Acknowledgements

I would like to thank my friend Frank Knowles, for copying photographs and improving them as if by magic. Also the late Dr R.G. Rowley and his wife, Val Rowley, for lending me their photographs, and reading and offering suggestions about the text.

Many people, whose help in previous publications has been invaluable in compiling this book, have now passed away so I would like to remember some of them here – the majority being Skipton born and bred: Mr Jack Inman, Mrs Gomersall, Paul McKay, Messrs E.B. and W.E. Thornton, Fred Manby, Miss Dagget, Mr R. and Miss Hyde, Mr P. Baldwin (former librarian), Mr Joe Wiseman and Sam Throup. Also Miss Smith, daughter of J.H. Smith, the photographer who took many of these photographs between 80 and 100 years ago.

I would also like to acknowledge more recent assistance given by: John Addyman, Peter Clarke, David Armitage, Ken Knowles, Raleigh Hargreaves, Charles Branston, John Phillip, Barbara Wood, Jim Tosney, Arthur Norton, Bryon Robinson, Mabel Hole, Brenda Shepherd, Miss Ruth Booth, Jack Longden, John Preston, Donald Binns, Mrs Barron, Ian Lockwood (*Craven Herald*) and Leslie Smith (former clerk to the Skipton Urban District Council).

Thanks finally to my daughter Dr Deborah K. Oates and my granddaughter Emily V. Oates for typing the manuscript.

The author with his wife, Kathleen, celebrates fifty-two years since he first flew this Tiger Moth while serving in the RAF, he even wears the same uniform! The celebration in 1998 coincided with the grant of an old 'A' licence for private pilots and four years' ownership of this Tiger Moth, R5172.

Introduction

My wife Kathleen and I came to live and work in Skipton in the spring of 1953. I was employed as the school Dental Surgeon and Kath followed to take up the post of Staff Nurse at Skipton General Hospital. We were not married then so I lodged at the Brick Hall (now the Woolly Sheep) and she in the nurses' home. We spent our free time walking and cycling (our only means of transport then) in and around Skipton, so we got to know it very well.

Among our first friends in Skipton were Dr Geoffrey Rowley and his wife Val. Together we collected or copied (with permission) a vast number of old photographs of Skipton and the surrounding area. In 1969 Geoff produced a history of Skipton and I followed in 1975 with *Skipton a Pictorial Recollection* and in 1982 *Life in Old Skipton* (both produced by Dalesman Books).

This book approaches Skipton from all directions, as we did cycling and on foot, using pictures taken over the past 100 years. No doubt the reader will recognise many features unchanged to this day. Once arrived at the town I will take you on a tour around the town centre in a bygone age, noting shops, vehicles, people and their activities. Many decades will be remembered, happy times and sad – a particularly poignant time being the years of war. Also included are photographs of Sir Alan Cobham's Flying Circus, who came to Sandylands in the late twenties and early thirties, pictures which I saw for the first time only in recent years.

The approach to Skipton from the south along the Keighley Road is interesting because it passes through the Aire Gap, with the Leeds to Carlisle railway and the River Aire on the left, and very near to the Leeds and Liverpool Canal (on the right). During the Second World War a Wellington bomber crashed on the narrow space between the canal and the road killing every member of the Polish crew. It was about three-quarters of a mile south of Bradley Lane End. We lived in Bradley for a while and spoke to eyewitnesses about the incident.

The people there are very friendly and we learnt a lot from them. We found that the old road from Keighley was high on the hillside from Kildwick, Farnhill and High Bradley. The road was built to avoid the valley bottom, which was liable to flooding. This route is on John Ogilby's map 'Oakham to Richmond', 1674. The folio of maps, produced at the express command of Charles II, was too big to carry so he produced a Traveller's Guide in 1699 and in it he referred to Skipton as 'indifferent, large and well built which has a good market on Saturdays'.

There were lovely green fields to the edge of Skipton which eventually became the site of the Snaygill Industrial Estate. I once walked with Sam Throup of High Bradley to his out-barn, which looked down on this and all he said was 'They're concreting old England ower'.

I hope that this book will prove to be a valuable record of our town's past as we approach the new Millenium.

Ken Ellwood
May 1999

Aerial view behind the castle, May 1994. Shown here is the towpath of Springs Canal, the church and the High Street. Deer roam in the woods, behind which there is a public footpath within only a five minute walk of the town.

One
Approach From Keighley

The railway from Skipton to Ilkley was constructed around 1885-87. Here we see the quite extensive bridge works to carry this line over the main line into Skipton, the Keighley Road and the Leeds to Liverpool Canal. Mouseley & Co. of Bristol was the contractor and the engineer was Charles Stansfield Wilson. His son Thornton Wilson, who lived in Bradley, showed me his diaries around 1957 and his great grandson, Anthony, loaned me the original photographs.

The visitor to Skipton approaching the town from Keighley around 1908 would have had to cross old Pinder Bridge, which took traffic over the Leeds and Liverpool Canal. 'Clogger' Thompson's shop can be seen on the left side of the bridge. The notices advertise early films at the Temperance Hall, now the Plaza Cinema.

During the period of demolition and reconstruction of the bridge a temporary footbridge was erected for pedestrians. Heavy vehicles had to use a diversion round by Cavendish Street. The builder was Braithwaite of Leeds who also built Carleton Road Bridge over the River Aire. Clerk of Works was Jim Smith of No.1 Thornton Street.

A canal trip, probably organised by the Rechabites. The new Pinder Bridge is under construction.

After completion the bridge was tested with three steamrollers and a traction engine being driven over it, in both directions, on 9 November 1910. Note the elegant street lamps on the south side of the bridge.

Joe Wiseman, brother of 'Old Bill' who founded the bus company and garage in Broughton Road, wrote a short history of Christ Church. The Earl of Thanet gave the site for the church and burial ground. Christ Church College Oxford, patrons of the living of Skipton, donated land and buildings in the town, part of the great tithes worth £1,200 as an endowment for the new church. The first stone was laid on 21 June 1837 and the building of the church was completed in September 1839.

Sackville Street joins Keighley Road near Pinder Bridge (to the right), *c.* 1914. The Temperance Hall stands where the Plaza Cinema is now.

Horner the butcher stands next to Sackville House which advertises apartments and accommodation for cyclists.

Looking back along Keighley Road the two carts illustrate the narrow point of the road, which was a consequence of the position of the old Unicorn Hotel. They all stand near the entrance to what is now the bus station. The wall on the left is the bridge parapet for Waller Hill Beck.

This cobbler's shop was opposite the wall of the Waller Hill Beck, seen on the previous picture. The beck is on the right. Mr Walker kept 'lasts' for fitting Craven gentlemen with boots and shoes; each customer had his own personal 'last'. His young assistant is Evelyn Hall who walked into work from Carleton each day.

This shop was near to the Star Inn yard. The picture is owned by Mrs Sheila Preston, a relative of the proprietors of Whincup's.

This shop adjoined the old Unicorn Hotel on part of the site which is now occupied by the After Dark nightclub, once the Regal Cinema.

In this part of Keighley Road the cattle fair often spilled out from the lower part of the High Street known then as Market Place and Caroline Square. The old Ship Hotel was demolished in the years between 1888 and 1890 to widen the narrow and dangerous Ship corner.

15

John Hogg was landlord of the Ship Hotel from 1874 to 1885. At this time Ship Corner was only 23 feet wide at its narrowest point. The building on the right housed Skipton post office. The arch was erected annually in celebration of the Craven Agricultural Society's Show.

A better view of the Ship Hotel, *c.* 1886. This was during the period of the incumbency of Francis Addyman, the last landlord of the Ship Hotel before it was demolished.

Before television one of the main sources of entertainment was the cinema. Pictured is the Regal Cinema in Keighley Road, along with various shops, in the 1960s.

The rebuilt Ship Hotel was a residential hotel until its closure in 1924. The building, however, saw many other uses, as we shall see in later photographs. In the floor of the doorway on the right there is, to this day, a mosaic which reads 'Ship Hotel'. 'Stabling' on the arch can also be detected.

The mosaic, pictured in January 1999.

A view looking back along Keighley Road to the Old Unicorn. Part of the house, which was Hargreaves' Dental Surgery, is on the left. This house and Shuttleworth's were demolished to make way for Burton's Buildings and road widening.

The fine looking house of Mr Hargreaves the dentist and the shop belonging to Shuttleworth the grocer are seen here being demolished.

Shuttleworth the grocer at No. 3 Keighley Road, next to Hargreaves the dentist.

A view of the new shops in the Ship Buildings and also Burton's Buildings. Note also the entrance to the Premier Cinema.

Next door to the cobbler's shop was the newspaper shop, umbrella hospital and barber's shop of Mr H. Lister. The *Daily Sketch* placard, 'Kitchener off to Egypt', dates the picture to 1896.

Two

Approach Along Broughton Road

Skipton Fire Brigade outside the Bull Inn at Broughton, 19 June 1905. They were returning from a mill fire at Earby. The tall man on the right is Walter Ellison of Ellison and Fawcett, who may have had the foundry before Varleys. Some of the others were from Smith and Chew, the carters, at the bottom of Raikes Road.

An aerial view of the western approach to Skipton bypass, under construction in 1979. Note the old Broughton Bridge and the new one, with girders stretched across the River Aire. Also visible is the bridge over the railway to Carlisle and, just off the picture, a new bridge crossing the Leeds Liverpool canal.

The first houses that would have been seen when travelling from the direction of Broughton are pictured along with the Primitive Methodist church known as 'towd tin tab'. It was erected in 1906 and is now a community centre. Just beyond this is a building which now houses a Cantonese restaurant.

William Wiseman founded Old Bill's Bus Services and later opened a larger garage on the opposite side of the road. They were Ford dealers though Volvo later took over. The garage has since closed.

The new Old Bill Garage which was built on land across the road.

In 1953 Ings School enjoyed a visit by the school dentist, J.K. Ellwood, and his assistant Miss Barbara Wood. Miss Wood poses with some of the patients outside the first dental caravan.

A group of children from the Broughton Road area prepare for Guy Fawkes Night before the First World War, c. 1910.

The Carleton road bridges under construction in the late 1880s. The main line to Carlisle passed under the centre and Broughton Road under the far right. Prior to this the road to Carleton had a level crossing.

A handsome coach and four outside the Midland Hotel, opposite Skipton Railway Station, c. 1908. This is now called Herriot's Hotel.

The old Auction Mart, which has now moved out past Aireville Park. Christ Church is in the distance. A Morrison's supermarket now occupies this site.

The new Skipton Auction Mart, situated next to the western bypass, opened in 1990. It is difficult to see from the road as it lies on top of a hill. The western bypass and Leeds to Liverpool Canal can also be seen.

Skipton station with a Midland locomotive in the horse dock siding. Rombald's Moor and Christ Church are in the background.

A Midland railway locomotive leaves Skipton southbound, *c.* 1900. It passes the Midland Hotel and Dewhurst's Mill.

The gentleman in the sidecar of this superb combination is Mr Hale, who worked for Midland Railway Co. as head of telegraphs at Skipton station from 1888 to 1915. He is pictured here in 1919.

The staff of Skipton railway station celebrate the Coronation year of King George V with a staff photograph. This postcard was printed as a Coronation souvenir and had a portrait of the King on the other side.

W.H. Smith & Sons occupied this book and newspaper stall on Skipton station. One headline reads 'Great fires caused by Antwerp strikers'. The *Daily News* has 'British blacklegs denounced at Labour congress'. The stationmaster is on the right.

A fine group of railwaymen at Skipton engine shed. Standing ready in steam is a Midland Railway express locomotive. Jack Barrow (uncle of Dr Geoffrey Rowley) is pictured on the back row, third from the right.

A Midland Railway locomotive with crew and cleaners.

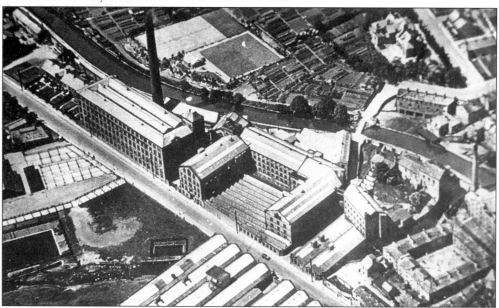

This aerial view shows the canal, Dewhurst's Mill, Union Square, the Auction Mart and the Skipton Cottage Hospital (top right), c. 1930.

Union Square was built in the early 1800s, with a top storey specifically provided for handloom weaving. There was also a 'selling out shop' within these walls to provide beer for the inhabitants. The square was demolished in 1956.

Some residents of Union Square in Back Bridge Street, around the time of the Coronation of King George VI. Among those pictured are: ? Mullarky, Mr Lever, Mrs Parks, Violet Tyson with baby Mary Tyson, Mrs McGowan, Mrs Hennigan, Kathleen Hennigan, Maria McGowan, Mrs Foley, Mrs Swales, Jimmy Lever, Jack Tyson. The two girls at the front are Totty Lever and Margaret Mullarky. The building in the background housed toilets and behind that was Victoria Mills (Tom Lumbs Paper Mill) which has since been converted into flats.

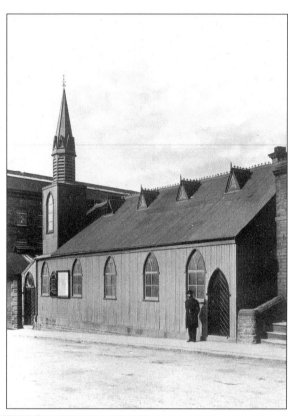

This is the Baptist chapel between Dewhurst's Mill and Belmont Bridge, which was in use from 1888 to 1915. It was destroyed by fire around 1920. The prefabricated building was supplied by William Harebrow from his works at Bermondsey in the south of England.

The Belmont Bridge area during the big flood of 1911. The canal here overflowed into the builder's yard of Thomas Duckett.

Over Belmont Bridge we find this view towards Ship Corner in the early 1900s. Note the footpath across the road which would be unmade. Swadforth (or Swadford) Street, is one of the oldest streets in the town, dating back to the fifteenth century. Its name derives from the ford that was once the crossing for Eller Beck.

This scene was captured during the flood of 1979. Unfortunately, the photographer arrived too late to see the landlord of the Cock and Bottle swim to the Co-op and back!

This float belonging to the Skipton Co-operative Society was a prizewinner in the Skipton Hospital Gala sometime in the early 1930s. Arthur Robinson poses with 'Dapple' behind the Co-op on Swadford Street.

The Gala Queen parades along Swadford Street in the late 1940s. The old folks rest centre changed its name to the Swadford Centre, no doubt to improve its image. The queen was Mavis Geldard.

One of the earliest pictures of Ship Corner, with Christ Church Vicarage on the right. A low wall surrounded the corner. The vicarage is still there but much altered. On the left there is a urinal at the rear entrance of the Brick Hall Inn, now called The Woolly Sheep Inn.

This rather better picture of the same area shows the low wall with railings on the right by the vicarage, *c.* 1886. Also pictured is the house belonging to Mr Hargreaves (the dentist), and the narrow entrance to Caroline Square.

Christ Church Vicarage was erected on land given by Skipton parish church for the endowment of the new Christ Church erected in 1837. The old Tithe Barn can be seen on the right. The vicarage was converted in 1901 to a block of shops, now known as Central Buildings.

The old Tithe Barn in its later years was used by travelling showmen and salesman. It was demolished in 1901 to make way for Mr A.R. Stockdale's Wine and Spirit Lodge. Originally it had a thatched roof, but this was removed in 1750 and re-covered with stone slates by Mr Thornton (a founder of the firm, R.Thornton and Sons, slaters who closed their business a few years ago). This photograph was taken just before the barn was demolished.

A wintry scene on Swadford Street. Two horse-drawn carts are present. Dewhurst's Mill chimney still dominates the scene.

Skipton Hospital Gala in 1911. This annual event began in 1900 and is still going strong.

Ship Corner arch, celebrating the Coronation of King George V in 1911. Mr Horner, a guard with the Midland Railway, stands to attention on the left. Through the archway are the Central Buildings, converted from the old Christ Church Vicarage – the line of the vicarage railings can still be found on the pavement.

Caroline Square looks enormous without the roundabout. The Ship Hotel is still in business and Wilson's saddlers shop is also present. Flight Sergeant John William Dunford was a grandson of the Wilsons. He was killed while serving with the RAF during the Second World War (see p. 125). The arch dates the picture as 1911.

The south side of Caroline Square, named after the unhappy wife of King George IV, shows the entrance to Queen's Court. Foster Horner, painter and plumber, occupied this shop from 1891 to 1973. 'Tinner' Wear had the adjoining shop. Woolworth's now occupies the left hand half of these buildings. On the building next to Woolworth's (which at present houses Superdrug) a plaque was placed by The Yorkshire Society to commemorate the birth of Thomas Spencer. It reads 'Born on this site, 1851, co-founder of Marks and Spencer'. To the left along Newmarket Street is another route into Skipton from Ilkley.

This dreadful scene was to be found behind buildings down Birtwhistle's Yard in 1979.

Midland Bank was built here in 1888; under its shoulder stands the tiny Wheatsheaf Inn.

The completed bridge over the unmade Broughton Road frames a view of the gasworks on Cavendish Street and the edge of Rombald's Moor. The house on the left, now demolished, was the stationmaster's house.

Three
Approach From Ilkley and Harrogate

This is the old road into Skipton called Shode or Shortbank Road, which runs down from the Roman road along Rombald's Moor. Sharphaw can be seen in the distance.

John Scott built the first indoor baths and also a house to live in, which is the present headquarters of the RAF Association. Only the latter can still be seen up Shortbank Road here in 1909. John Scott was an early entrepreneur, he had an antique shop at the present Masonic Hall in Sackville Street and when this failed he turned his hand to selling pie and peas in the hall. He let the baths go to Skipton Urban District Council.

Mrs E. Etty has lived in Duckett Street all her life. She provided these photographs of her grandfather, John Scott, who is seen here (top left) with the swimming club.

Harry Scott is about to dive in on the right. Many Skipton people will remember the interior of the baths. Harry was father of Mrs Etty and son of John Scott who built the baths.

The tower built for high diving is decorated for the Coronation in 1911.

At one time John Scott and his wife Margaret lived in the old Toll Bar at the bottom of Shortbank Road, which also had sulphur springs. Margaret charged a penny a glass for this water.

The Ancient Free Grammar School of Skipton in Craven. A plaque above the door reads 'This sixteenth-century building was originally the Chapel of St James of the Knights Hospitallers of St John of Jerusalem. It subsequently passed into the hands of Canon Ermysted who housed his Grammar School here, which he founded in 1548'. It is now used as an electricity sub station.

The Skipton Prize Band lead a parade along Newmarket Street. They have been slowed down by the conductor for the photograph to be taken, in the 1920s. The Cross Keys is on the left and the Nags Head on the right.

The whole of this south side of Newmarket Street has now disappeared. Among the shops stood a once stately mansion known as Newmarket House (a three-storey building) which ended its days as a model lodging house. At one time the Circuit Judge stayed here. The building was demolished in 1957.

Almost next door to the telephone exchange stands the Congregational church, now known as St Andrew's church. John Edward Gaunt, Miss Gunnell, John Harrison and Thomas Henry Dewhurst laid the memorial stones of the church on 19 September 1914.

Some of the buildings just a short distance from the High Street have long since gone. Stanley House in Newmarket Street, pictured here, was demolished to make way for the post office telephone exchange.

When Otley Street was opened out in the early 1840s, the first building to be erected was the Albion Inn, which took over the licence of the old Butcher's Arms Inn in Spring Gardens, Otley Road. In common with most of the inns of Skipton it passed into the hands of Scott and Robinson's Skipton Brewery.

Just off Otley Street was the British School. Paul McKay provided this picture; he became a mill engineer and part-time gamekeeper in Skipton Woods. He helped George Leatt to restore the mill wheel and machinery in the Corn Mill, Chapel Hill. Ellesmere Press is now in the British School building.

There is a narrow alleyway called the Ginnel, which leads from Newmarket Street down the side of the Quaker's Meeting House to a pretty area through which runs Waller Hill Beck. The Civic Society formed a scheme to improve this area, including the provision of a footpath alongside the beck to connect with Keighley Road via Devonshire Place. The path had to cross the beck so society member Jim Wales, a local architect, designed a bridge which was constructed by third and fourth year Aireville School pupils, ably led by crafts master Tom Pettit. It was displayed at the Great Yorkshire Show as a Jubilee project and the Duke of Edinburgh spoke to the boys while they were working to finish it off. The boys erected the bridge in 1978. The Civic Society still take an interest in this area.

The site of Dyneley House can be traced through title deeds to John Lambert of Calton. In 1745 the house was conveyed to Edward Dyneley and in a Skipton valuation of 1840 the resident was John Dyneley. J.B. Dewhurst lived here from 1851 to 1866 followed by Col. George Robinson, general manager of Craven Bank. His son George Geoffrey Robinson was born here on 25 October 1874, he later changed his surname to Dawson and became editor of *The Times*. By 1955 the house was in use as a private hotel. It was demolished in the 1960s and the site is now occupied by doctors' surgeries.

Skipton postal workers. They are assembled on the beautiful lawn behind Dyneley House. This is a good illustration of the fashions at the time, particularly those fashions pertaining to ladies hats.

'The Best Man for Coal'. Another businessman who lived in Newmarket Street was Frank Whalley, coal merchant, seen here getting ready for Skipton Gala.

In Newmarket Street are the premises of T.L. Frearson, ironmongers. This shop along with Manby Bros in the High Street will be remembered by many as a wonderful emporium. The Skipton Building Society occupied the adjoining building, towards the right of the picture.

Having arrived back in Caroline Square we now look at the road from Harrogate, which enters Skipton at the top of High Street down the Bailey alongside the castle. This picture shows Fattorini's Corner which was erected in 1863 by Mr Baldisaro Porri for his son-in-law, Mr Innocent Fattorini the jeweller. The adjoining property was demolished in 1895 and now forms part of High Street House.

The Annual Show in 1896 (by D. Brownsworth, Otley Street). The field was beyond the Bailey to the left of the Embsay road. Embsay crag can be seen in the distance. This field was also used for Skipton Gala until it moved to Aireville Park. In the deeds it is called the 'Storems' which has some association with deer. John Addyman, who owns the field, says the walls are very high so deer may have been kept here, to be near Skipton Castle.

This road, which joins the top of the High Street, is called The Bailey and follows the castle wall. It features on Ogilby's strip map of 1674, York to Lancaster.

Before the Second World War the visitor to Skipton from Harrogate might have seen two saddle-tank locomotives hauling limestone wagons alongside the road from the direction of Hawbank Quarry. They would pass under a bridge carrying the road branching off to Embsay and then to the top of the incline behind Skipton Castle. *Wyvern* was eventually sold to Balfour Beatty & Co.

This bridge carried the road to Embsay. The track bed of the railway which ran parallel to the Harrogate road can be seen here on the right. This bridge is not far from the top of the incline down which the wagons were lowered by a system seen in the next picture.

The wagons from the quarry were lowered down to the canal by means of a wire rope controlled by a brake. The loaded wagons pulled up the empties, the two passed at the halfway point seen here.

Mr Hyde was in charge of the incline system and lived in this charming cottage, now in ruins.

An empty barge stands ready to receive stone from the wagons by way of the chutes.

On 1 May 1962 there was a trial loading with a view to using barges again. The rail track had been taken up long ago so a lorry was used to carry the stone down the old incline.

Four

Approach From Gargrave and Grassington

A most popular fish and chip van belonging to Holmes and Willis of Grassington visited villages north of Skipton. Willis are now going strong in removals and storage and are situated to the west of Skipton on the bypass.

Aireville Swimming Pool under construction in 1963. Anita Lonsbrough, an Olympic swimmer, officially opened the pool in May 1964. A new pool is now being planned on a slightly different site.

The road from Gargrave and the west originally passed through Thorlby and Stirton and down Raikes Road, as shown in Ogilby's strip map, York to Lancaster, 1674. The main road now passes Aireville Park, as shown here. The pavement was then known as 'The Promenade'.

A view of Salisbury Street before it was extended as Raikeswood Road through to Raikes Road. Note the fence dividing the street from the old quarry (now the site of Skipton Girls High School tennis courts) and the woods above.

This area of Skipton was photographed from the air, c. 1930. The photographer was perhaps Earl Fielden who flew with Sir Alan Cobham's flying circus. He lived in the area near Raikes Avenue. Salisbury Street is on the left and Raikes Road and Grassington Road are at the top. Lower down is Skipton workhouse, which was later a hospital and is now Gainsborough Court.

The old coach road is on the left coming from the direction of Gargrave, Thorlby and Stirton in the early 1900s. The original route is shown in Ogilby's strip map, York to Lancaster. Grassington Road is on the right and is shown in Ogilby's strip map, Oakeham to Richmond.

Skipton Cottage Hospital in Granville Street (seen here in the early 1900s) was eventually used as council offices. This building was demolished because of dry rot. Pine Close is now situated here.

Skipton. Girls' Endowed Schools.

Skipton Girls High School before many alterations and extensions took place. The building on the right accommodated girls who boarded at the school.

44736. SKIPTON: BOYS GRAMMAR SCHOOL

Ermysted's Grammar School (see p. 44). For a complete history of this school the reader should refer to a history written by A.M. Gibbon, MA (Oxon) entitled *The Ancient Free Grammar School of Skipton in Craven*, published in 1947.

59

This Primitive Methodist chapel was demolished to make way for a block of flats.

Gargrave Road before Park Avenue was built. The Primitive Methodist chapel is on the left and St Stephen's School on the right.

This was the first Primitive Methodist chapel, being in use from 1835 to 1880. Later it housed Bishop and Schroot's cycle shop and then, until 1974, was the home of Skipton Fire Station. It is now the Craven College Academy for Hair and Beauty Therapy.

Lower Commercial Street, *c.* 1960, looking down towards the old fire station – now Craven Academy for Hair and Beauty Therapy. All except the latter have now been demolished and the site is now a car park.

The Allotment Gardener's Association show for the Skipton Hospital Gala of 1911, outside the Joiners Arms in Lower Commercial Street.

William IV hostelry in Water Street.

Behind the gala float is the printing works of Edmondson & Co. Thomas Edmondson was born on 21 August 1837 and his mother died when he was only nine years old. In his own words he 'became a farm man for my granny at Greenhow Hill'. He returned to Skipton at the age of fifteen and was apprenticed to Mr Tasker, who had a printing business in the premises now occupied by the *Craven Herald*. On completing his indenture he continued to work for some years as a journeyman printer and had made plans for entering into partnership as master printer at Keighley. However, Mr John Dawson, founder of the *Skipton Pioneer* asked him to join his business and Thomas became the active partner in starting and building up the printing, publishing and stationery business of Edmondson & Co.

Skipton Urban District Council Wallis steamroller in the 1930s. This scene is at a time when rough roads were being surfaced with small stones bound by tar. Coach Street Bridge is behind and to the right. Beyond is the Royal Shepherd.

The steamroller would be heading for the Skipton UDC depot, *c.* 1922. Included among the roadmen working for the council were: Bernard Mullarkey, John Ingham, Steven Reeder, Alf Watson, John Nutter, Tommy Reynolds.

Over the bridge along Coach Street was the shop of T. Farnell, picture framer and wood carver. The shop is seen here decorated for the Coronation of King George V. H.C. Foster learned his trade as a wood carver and picture framer from Mr Farnell and took over the business but moved to premises across the road. This shop is now The Green Room, Organic Hairdressers.

Mr Foster and assistant Kathleen Atkins, with Master Maroney whose parents had a shoe shop nearby. Mr Foster retired in 1961. Some of his work can be found in the chapel of Skipton parish church, Holy Trinity.

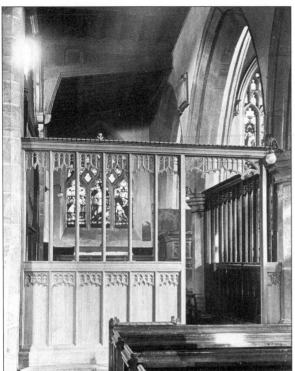

Mr Foster carved this screen in Holy Trinity Church.

Another fine example of wood carving by Mr Foster. Where is it now?

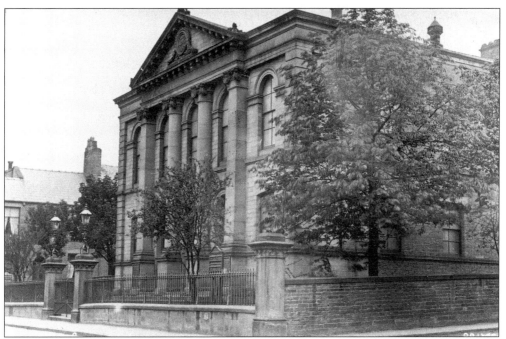

The Wesleyan chapel in Water Street, built in 1864. This is now the Registrar's Office and the exterior has recently been cleaned. This building was used in the mid-1950s for Youth Employment, Education and Health Offices.

Most of these girls worked at the Health Centre at the top of the High Street. They are, from the left: Nora Dodd, Beryl Eastwood, Barbara Coates, Barbara Wood, Joan Knowles, Bessie Riley, Mary Harris, Bessie Baker, Sheila Dale, Betty Mee and Louise Simpson.

Phillip and Sons, family butchers near Back Water Street, c. 1903. The *Craven Herald* office can be seen over John Phillip's head. The youngest boy, his son, is the father of the present John Phillip of Newmarket Street. The other boy is Richard Phillip.

A working farm in the heart of Skipton, at the bottom of Raikes Road. Holy Trinity church is in the background. The farm was operational until the 1960s but is now a private residence. The steamroller is a Ruston and belonged to West Riding County Council. It stands next to the Pinfold where stray beasts were kept to be returned on payment of a fine. On the corner, just behind the two men is a blacksmith's shop owned by Mr Jack Ward. This is now the premises of Bob Wright's Wine Shop.

The same steamroller and a better view of the barn, next to Raikes farm, with hay inside. This is also a private residence now, separate to the one converted from the farmhouse.

A West Riding steamroller, by Ruston of Lincoln rolls a mix of tar and small stones at the junction of Raikes Road and Gargrave Road. Notice also the tar boiler that Ermysted's boys are watching and an Old Bill's Motors wagon beyond.

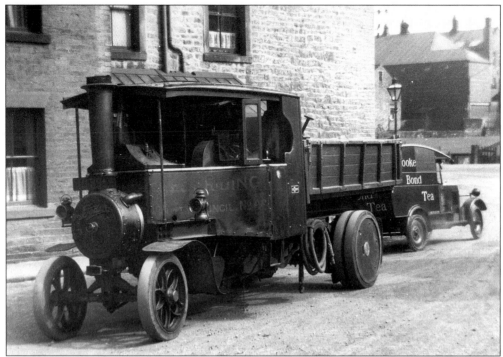

A West Riding Council Foden wagon stands at the bottom of Raikes Road. It would be a support vehicle for the steamrollers.

The houses behind the postman, at the bottom of Raikes Road, were demolished in 1956. Springs Canal and Eller Beck run under Mill Bridge. Notice that there is a boy clinging on half-way up an attractive lamp-post.

The New Ship next to Springs Canal and Mill Bridge. In 1918 Fred Alderson lived here with his family. Tom Clark, gamekeeper to Skipton Castle, is seen returning from a foxhunt on Crookrise.

A three horsepower charabanc outside the Castle Inn, *c.* 1900. A furniture sale is advertised outside the New Ship – the auctioneer is perhaps Mr Alderson.

No book showing this part of Skipton would be complete without a photograph of Stanforths Celebrated Pork Pie Establishment. Taken around 1974 the picture also shows Amy Eagan's antique shop.

Five

High Street and
Sheep Street

Before moving up the High Street and Middle Row take a look at this aerial photograph from 1949. Burton's Buildings, the Regal Cinema, Swadford Street and Keighley Road are at the bottom of the picture and the church and castle are at the top. Many buildings, such as those in Albert Street, have now gone and the area has been redeveloped.

Across the square William Hogg had a fish, fruit, game and ice shop there from 1892 to 1903. This was 100 High Street and the '100' was painted next to Hogg. It could still be seen up to a few years ago, even after it had been painted over many times.

The lower section of Middle Row, c. 1875. The National Westminster Bank occupies the whole of the Exchange Buildings now. The three shops were occupied by Andrew the ironmonger, the *Craven Pioneer* and 'Staffordshire House', which was John Metcalfe's furniture and china shop.

The men who reported the news. The editorial and advertising staff of the *Craven Herald* and the former *West Yorkshire Pioneer*, prior to the two weekly Skipton newspapers' amalgamation in the 1930s. From left to right, back row: Stanley Senior, Harry Watson, Roland Eames, Albert Mitchell, Robert Brayshay, John Mitchell. Front row: Billy Noake, Noel Wild, Rob Scott, Raynor Garbutt, Charles Branston, Fred Aldridge (photographer).

No. 90 High Street. William Mattock the corn merchant occupied these premises, down the steps was Mrs Keighley's eating house. William Mattock also had the High Corn Mill.

Through the arch from Sheep Street was one of Skipton's typical yards, now demolished. This was Albert Street, now it leads to an area of very nice shops. The shop seen here belonged to Mr Sedgwick the photographer.

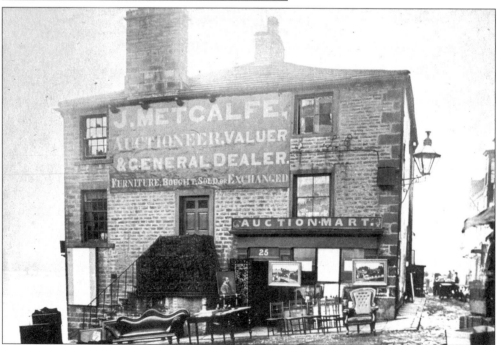

John Metcalfe's furniture shop on Sheep Street Hill was demolished in 1895 to make way for Exchange Buildings. Temperance speakers used to address the passers by from the top of the steps.

During the 1920s all the local buses used this lower part of the High Street as a bus station.

Caroline Square was still being used as a bus station in the 1930s.

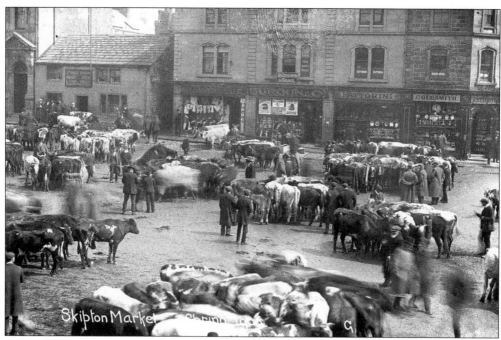

Skipton's fortnightly cattle fair was held in the main streets on alternate weeks until 1906, when after thirty years of argument it was moved to Jerry Croft, now the carpark at the rear of the town hall. Within two years of the market moving out of the streets three High Street Inns had closed – the Thanet's Arms, the Fountain and the Wheatsheaf (pictured here).

OLD SKIPTON

This rhyme was written by Herbert Wilkes, the Skipton postman-poet, towards the end of the last century, when all the public houses named (except those in the last two verses) were flourishing. The Bay Horse was the first to close, in 1898.

There's my Black Horse, he'll face the Lion,
And make the Bay Horse fly:
He'll turn the Wheatsheaf upside down,
And drink the Fountain dry.

He'll leave a mark upon the Fleece,
Take shine out of the Star,
And make King William sue for peace
Before the Castle Bar.

He'll crush the Midland on his tour,
And make the Shepherd scream;
Despatch Commercials any hour
To Devonshire for cream.

He'll twist the Cross Keys out of shape,
And fill the Nag with dread;
The Albion shall not escape;
The Hart must lose its head.

He'll make the New Ship spring a leak.
Give Craven Arms a jerk.
And make the King's afraid to speak
When Joiners are at work.

He'll straighten up the Rose and Crown,
The Royal Oak must fall,
He'll knock the Cock and Bottle down,
And close the Hole in't Wall.

He'll slip the Thanets down a nick,
And make the Heifer grin;
Then canter off and throw the "Brick"
Beyond the Railway Inn.

He'll make the Craven look forlorn,
And strain Old George's lip,
Destroy the boasting Unicorn,
And then upset the Ship.

He'll make the White Horse scrape and bow,
The Jolly Sailors fight,
The Mason's Arms will strike a blow
Before the Sun is bright.

He'll trample on the Woodman's score,
T' Black Bull will turn away,
And fight alone will save the Swan
Before he meets his day.

Pubs of Skipton.

The Hole in the Wall was a popular pub, which closed its doors in 1976 and became part of Craven Court. These charabancs are very rare now. This occasion is no doubt a pub outing.

The earliest known photograph of Skipton shows the High Street on the occasion of Skipton Show, the annual exhibition of the Craven Agricultural Society, which was held from 1855 to 1929.

This must be about twenty years after the previous picture of Skipton Show; Midland Bank (built in 1888) can be seen on the right, but the trees, which were to be planted in 1897 are not yet in evidence. Note the two footpaths across the unmade road and Scott the tub-maker's shop on the left.

The Wheat Sheaf Inn in the High Street closed in 1908. Squire Firth was a keen brass bandsman, as is the present Squire Firth who provided the photograph.

The state of the streets on wet market days was one factor which led to agitation for the removal of the market elsewhere. Skiptonians would not go shopping on market days so what the innkeepers gained the shopkeepers lost.

High Street, showing the areas marked off for the assembly of the different denominations who took part in the Whit Walk, for example PM is for the Primitive Methodists.

On 27 April 1897, the council decided to commemorate the Diamond Jubilee of Queen Victoria by planting trees in the High Street. Mr George Harrison Mason, who founded the well known firm of G.H. Mason & Sons, was the chairman of the committee responsible for making the arrangements. The lime trees arrived from Carlisle on 9 November 1897, and planting began on the following day. A tree can be seen lying on the stone setts awaiting planting.

Sheep Street before the First World War. Sheep Street is split off from the High Street by Middle Row. Some of the shops on this side of the High Street are worth recording.

82

'Forts' drapers shop, Sheep Street, in 1905. Arthur, then eighteen, had just left Ermysted's to join his mother and father in the family business. The lady shown is one of the shop assistants. Due to his illness the shop was sold to Mr Atkinson of Leeds in 1947. It continued as a ladies outfitters and now is Greenwood's mens' outfitters.

Lipton the grocer displays a mouth-watering selection of fare in an era long before the supermarket.

Phillip the butcher and G.H. Mason the plumber occupied these shops on the site of the old Black Bull Inn, later the Sun Inn. The shops were demolished and rebuilt for G.H. Mason & Son in 1928 and are now occupied by Boots the Chemist.

Sheep Street in the 1950s. Compare this with the way the street looks today.

The oldest family business in the High Street was Fred Manby & Bros, established here in 1817 (now occupied by Jumper). Lower down Middle Row is the Fountain Inn.

An illustration of Edwardian fashions. The year is 1902 when Edward VII was crowned, and this is Dewhurst's float in the gala, which in those days travelled from Gargrave Road and down the High Street.

The funeral procession on 18 November 1920, of the victims of the Barrowford charabanc disaster. Five young Skipton men, aged between sixteen and twenty-two, were killed in the accident, which occurred on the way to a football match. The driver was charged with drunken driving but was found not guilty. A Rolls Royce can be seen outside Amblers shop. Also visible is a cart with beer barrels near to Old George Hotel.

Queen Mary had a great love of antiques and whenever she stayed at Harewood House, the home of the Princess Royal, she enjoyed visiting the most important dealers in the vicinity. Mr Laycock had a tremendous reputation in the world of antiques, as shown by this photograph of the Queen's visit to his shop in the High Street around 1930.

This Burrell traction engine, belonging to J.K. Ellwood, led the annual Round Table Santa Claus Parade to the town hall most years during the 1970s. Jim Turnbull of High Bradley is steering while Peter Ellwood rides in the coalbunker.

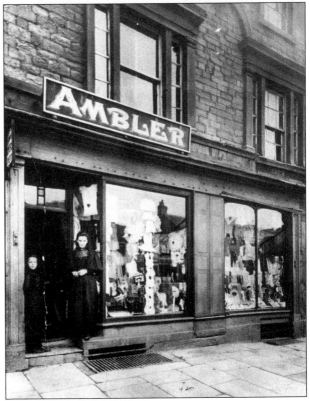

Mrs Ambler Ltd, 37 High Street, a milliner and ladies' and children's outfitter. Mrs Ambler started the business in 1893, selling high-class millinery, gowns, coats, hosiery and underwear. In 1961 the shop was taken over by Brown Muff's of Bradford and they extended the premises to the rear. In 1970 they took over the Old George, demolishing the rear but keeping the existing High Street façade. The shop is now Rackhams.

These eight charabancs appear to be packed full of children and they know they are being photographed! The car outside the Red Lion looks like a Model T Ford.

The garage of the Craven Motor Company in the 1920s. The *Craven Herald* buildings were on the right, now occupied by Thornton's chocolate shop.

A good view of the paved footpath, constructed to help people cross the unmade road which would be a mess on wet days and cattle market days. Here it is seen during the Coronation celebrations of 1911.

The cattle fair took over the whole of the High Street. On the right, in this study from the top end of the street from around 1900, is Mr James Reeday of Hetton who was eighty years of age when he died in 1914.

Statue of Sir Mathew Wilson, with the vicarage footpath to the left, sometime after the First World War. The Marquis of Ripon unveiled the statue of Skipton's first MP Sir Mathew Wilson, Bart., of Eshton hall in 1888. It was perhaps unusual that the statue was erected during his lifetime.

The statue was moved in 1921 by B.B. Kirk, builder and contractor, of Waller Hill. Mr Kirk (in the straw hat) stands with M. Baynes and others. The house in the background (now David Goldie's shop) was the home and surgery of Dr Forsyth Wilson and the birthplace in 1882 of his son, Charles MacMoran Wilson, who was to become Lord Moran, Sir Winston Churchill's personal physician.

90

Left: The statue was moved to make way for a cenotaph, a temporary wooden structure being erected on the site until a permanent one in stone could be constructed. *Right*: A model of the new cenotaph.

A rare picture of the hand-pump fire engine on the setts in front of the town hall. Grant Salisbury, who was a fire officer with the Skipton Station provided this photograph.

A fine house at the corner of the High Street and the road leading to Skipton's present car park. Claire Whitaker's shop with café above now occupies the site, with Threshers wine shop next door in place of Dobson the chemist. One of the young lime trees can be seen.

The High Street is seen from the church tower on Coronation Gala Day, June 1953. This perhaps shows dignitaries arriving before the parade.

This photograph of the Coronation Gala Queen was taken by George Prochok, a Ukranian who became a displaced person during the Second World War. He lodged for a time at the Brick Hall, from where this scene is pictured. He returned home to the Ukraine in 1954 and trained as a teacher. He later married and had a son. He died in 1997.

Holy Trinity church with the tombstones and graveyard in front. The tombstones were removed in the 1950s.

The West Gallery, now removed.

Archdeacon Cook with the bells of the church of Holy Trinity after they were recast by Messrs Taylor & Co. of Loughborough in 1921. They were rededicated on 12 August 1921. Dr Digby Burton is the present leader and will no doubt be ringing on into the Millennium.

The parish church choir, *c.* 1969. The head boy was Richard Henry Day and prominent among the adults is the popular choirmaster John Brown, head of music at Ermysted's Grammar School. Present also are curate John Berch, Joe Wiseman and Mr Mashiter a member and past president of the Craven Naturalist Society.

A view of the road down the Bailey as Skipton Gala parade enters the top of the High Street from Gargrave Road and Water Street. The statue of Sir Mathew Wilson was moved after the First World War to make way for the cenotaph. Note the wide area of cobbles and the old motor car.

A further view of the gala at the time of the Coronation celebrations in 1911. Of particular interest are the old cottages between High Street House (now a solicitor's office) and the vicarage. These cottages were demolished to make way for the Health Centre.

Through the gateway of the castle one met this attractive view of the old castle, with the Tudor wing attached. The wing was specially built as a residence for Henry Lord Clifford on his marriage with Lady Eleanor Brandon, granddaughter of King Henry VII.

Six

Sport

SKIPTON RUGBY F.C.

Sport has always played a large part in the life of Skipton and most sports are well represented. This team, led by Christopher Tosney, won the Yorkshire Challenge Cup 1911/12. To his right is A.M. Macintosh, headmaster of Ermysted's Grammar School. On his left is Alf Clarke who played trombone with the Skipton Mission Band. He would march with the band to Sandylands, change for the game and then march back to Skipton. The president today is Harry Crabtree who announced recently that this year (1999) the club would be 125 years old. There will be celebrations and fund raising events to improve the ground and clubhouse. Left to right, back row: J.C. McIntyre, J. Pickard, J. Graham, W. Fletcher, P. Fields, S. Bishop, H. Blakey. Middle Row: A. Lambert, A.M. Macintosh, C. Tosney (captain), A. Clark, W. Scott. Front Row: C. Thwaites, W. Brayshaw, J.E. Gill, G. Fennerty.

The Ermysted's Grammar School rugby team for the year 1938/39. Mr Beattie is on the left. He was the chemistry master and was very popular, nicknamed 'Wab' (his initials). Included in the photograph are three RAF pilots: Bob Turnbull, R.G.B. Summers OBE and David Smith, a long serving member of Skipton Golf Club. From left to right, top row: G. Heslop, J. Smith, Bob Turnbull, Norman Hodgon. Middle row: Austin Beattie, C.G. Suddards, Owen Brown, E. Procter, P.G. Hepworth, J.G. Lewis, R.G.B. Summers, J.H.S. Davey. Front row: David Smith, Maurice Hartley, Wyn Gray, D.H. Green, G. Hall.

Ermysted's Grammar School Cricket XI 1930/31. From left to right, back row: Maurice Hoare, Louis Tasker, ? Weston, Edwin Butt, Geoff (Titch) Cooper, ? Williamson. Front row: F.S. (Yankee) Wilson, Johnny Hoare, Stanley (York) Mason, Clifford Berry, Raleigh Hargreaves. Cap wearers: Half colours. Blazer wearer: Full colours (captain).

Skipton Rugby Union team in 1937. From left to right, back row: Ralph Hannam, -?- (referee), John Smallwood, Vincent Tosney, Preston James, Geoff Dixon, Maurice Friend, Tom Roberts, Dickie Ideson. Front row: Eric Bramfitt, Edgar Leach, Albert Horner, Jim Tosney, Stanley Mason, Tom Crowther, Fred Hurst. Albert Horner played many times for Yorkshire. Many of these chaps served in the war. Geoff Dixon was killed while flying a Liberator with Coastal Command. Jim Tosney served first with the Army, escaping from France south west of Dunkirk and later as a pilot with the RAF. Edgar Leach MBE also escaped from France with Jim.

The team which beat the Wasps when they were on tour. Left to right, back row: Raynor Garbut, Norman Hodgson, John Macmorland, Jim Tosney, Bill Peyton, Brian Swainson, Donald Cooban, Ken Schoon, Peter Mason, Frank Wellock, John Dodgson. Front row: William Preston, Charlie Branston, Arthur Norton, John Davey, Brian Atkinson. John Dodgson played for Yorkshire on sixteen occasions.

The 1951/52 Skipton Rugby Union team. From left to right, top row: Donald Cooban, Mike Anson, John Simpson, Brian Atkinson, Mickey Bell, Ray Walker, Willy Windle. Middle Row: Dick Middleton, B.E. Walls, Bill Jones, Dr G. Dick, Alan Baker, David Thornton, Brian Swaison, Stanley Peffer (treasurer). Bottom row: Frank Wellock, Tom Garnett, Wally Evans, Edgar Leach, Geoff Fisher.

Skipton Ladies' Hockey Team, *c.* 1969. Left to right, back row: E. Alden, S. Wiseman, J. Pilkington, L. Batchelor, C. Clarkson, K.M. Ellwood (secretary and president), A. Caton, E. Coombe. Front row: S. Atkins, M. Sutcliffe, M. Livock, R. Ratclife, A. Tattersall.

Well-dressed bowlers at Craven Bowling Club, next to the car park behind the town hall.

An Edwardian cricket scene at Skipton Cricket Club. Rombald's Moor is in the background.

Skipton Cricket Club in 1908, when they were winners of the Yorkshire Council by drawing almost all matches. Left to right, back row: Jack Smith of Carleton, O. Hall, Norman Robinson, Dan Robinson. Centre row: -?-, Foster Horner, Billy Greenwood (captain), Harry Gerald, Freddie Furness. Front row: Arthur Girling (professional groundsman), Howarth Watson.

Two celebrities visited Skipton in the 1930s. Bosanquet (the small man with bat), inventor of the 'googley', and Faulkner of South Africa.

Seven

Music

Forerunner of the Skipton Brass Band was Jack Guy's Band, seen here next to the bowling green behind The Devonshire. Jack Guy is on the far right.

Fred Metcalfe was the most famous of all Skipton Band conductors. He was a member of the Skipton Mission in which the band had its roots. He was quite a young man when he was appointed a bandmaster, a position he held until his death in 1930. He is seen here with 'young Fred', his son Fred Lloyd Metcalfe, who succeeded his father to serve the band for many years.

Many members of the band served in the First World War. When they returned some of them began to complain about the name 'Mission Band' as they felt that this gave them a poor image. So in 1919 the name was changed to Skipton Prize Band. In 1927 Fred Metcalfe took them to Crystal Palace where they won the *Daily Mirror* Trophy.

By the late 1960s the fortunes of the band were low and a big effort was launched to recruit new members. Money was raised to have the instruments converted to low pitch and then the professional and business people of Skipton were asked to contribute money to purchase new instruments. The band president Ken Ellwood set the ball rolling by presenting a new cornet. Deborah Ellwood is seen here making the presentation to principal cornet Wilbur Paley, a master of Ermysted's Grammar School. John Beck is on the left, Ken Bright is the conductor, and Ken Ellwood looks on.

The third instrument acquired was a euphonium, seen here with Ken Davy. Ken Bright is on the left with John Preston, secretary. John Preston and his wife Margaret worked extremely hard to keep the band going.

The Ladies Committee also worked extremely hard for the band and are seen here presenting two cornets, worth about £80 each. Today they would cost between £500 and £800 each. From left to right: Mrs K. Ellwood, Mrs Murray, Mrs B. Beck, Mrs M. Preston, Mrs Lawson, Mrs Bright. Trevor Greenwood is receiving a soprano cornet.

The band raised a tremendous amount of money by events such as this, a 'march and play' through thirty villages.

In the mid-1970s Ken Bright took the band to play on the old bandstand at Hardraw Force in Wensleydale, a natural amphitheatre. By coincidence the famous contest named after the site was soon to be revived and, ably led by Michael Norcross, conductor, Skipton Band won. They were victorious again the following year.

Ken Bright, the conductor of the Skipton Band, retired in 1974 and a presentation was made to him at the RAFA Club. From left to right, top row: Mike Jackson (chairman), Ken Ellwood (president), Ken Bright, Mrs Bright, John Preston (secretary). Middle row: John Yarker, John Ellwood, Andrew Cleaver, Ken Lee, Carol Scott, Anthony Davis. Bottom row: Ian Humphries, Steve Waltson, Michael Boothman, David Preston.

The complete band, fully uniformed and with mainly new instruments, pose in the grounds of Skipton Castle to celebrate the Queen's Silver Jubilee in 1977.

Before discos, music for dancing was live and dance bands played well into the night at most Craven towns and villages. This is Fred Hudson's Band, which was formed around 1949 and continued into the '50s. They played at Dewhurst's Welfare and the Clifford Hall in the Black Horse. Fred Hudson also played cornet with Cononley Band. From left to right, top: Fred Hudson, Keith Horner, Andy Hoe, Ralph Hudson, Arthur Dransfield, Cyril Williams, Bobby Horner, Jack Bean. Front: Alf Spence, Jack Longden, Lew Rawcliffe, Fred Thompson, Eric Butterfield, Billy Coe, Wendy Tennant (vocalist).

This is the successful Aireville School Band trained by the music master, Doug Shearer. Ermysted's Grammar School also had a very good brass band and orchestra. The success of the Skipton Band was partly due to many of these youngsters playing with the band. The school bands benefitted by the boys and girls using Skipton Band instruments.

The Billy Coe Seven came along after Fred Hudson and they played in the town hall. From left to right, top: Kenny Bell, Cyril Day, Billy Coe, Jeffrey Willis. Front: Dennis Bamber, Jack Wood, Jack Longden.

Eight
Aviation

The 1920s and '30s were a great time for British aviation. The minds of the public were captured by the feats of the Royal Flying Corps and the aviation companies were building lots of different aircraft to establish small airlines and provide aircraft for the private owner. Ex-RFC pilots purchased war surplus aircraft and set off round the country giving air displays from farm fields near to towns. One great aviator who came to Skipton was Sir Alan Cobham with his Flying Circus. Sandylands and Niffany were favourite sites. He also employed Earl Fielden, a well-known pilot whose parents had a shop in Swadford Street. Earl Fielden is pictured on the right of Sir Alan Cobham. On the far right is Walshaw Bateman, also of Skipton, who was an expert mechanic. Walshaw lived in Raikes Road in his retirement. In front of him is relative Freddie Kent who lived to be ninety-five. He was present at the first powered aeroplane flight in Britain and as an aircraft engineer worked with Amy Johnson, Jean Batten, Jim Mollison and Imperial Airways. He was an apprentice at the Royal Aircraft establishment at Farnborough and worked on the Be 2c, Fe 2B and SE5 the famous First World War fighter.

Skipton, October 1932. On the left is Avro 504 K G-EBYW of Aviation Tours. On the right is Handley Page W 8b G-EBB1, owned by Imperial Airways but used during 1932 by Earl Fielden of Aviation Tours Ltd and flown by him with Cobham. The moor above Kildwick is on the left and the moor above Carleton is on the right.

Earl Fielding of Skipton with some passengers boarding the Handley Page G-EBB1 named *Prince Henry*. Note the dress of the period. This aircraft was powered by two 360 horsepower Rolls Royce Eagle VIII engines.

Comper Swift G-ABPY, built in 1931 and first owned by National Aviation Day Ltd, was fitted with a radio and performed 'request' acrobatics under direction from the crowds. Eventually it was sold to Australia. It is seen here at Skipton on 21 June 1932. Note the well-dressed family looking on.

Airspeed A.S.4 Ferry prototype G-ABS1 *Youth of Britain II* joyriding with Cobham's National Aviation Displays Ltd at Skipton on 21 June 1932. On this visit Sir Alan Cobham addressed the Rotarians during their weekly lunch and suggested that all towns including Skipton should have an airfield.

National Aviation Day displays DH82 Tiger Moth G-ABUL, which was first registered in March 1932 and is seen at Skipton on 21 June of that year.

'Darling I shan't be long, just going for a quick spin.' Earl Fielden boards *Prince Henry*.

Clarence Robinson Merrill, Skipton Rural District Council's steamroller driver, was, according to his son, an aviation enthusiast. He stands by the Avro 504K during the tour's visit to Skipton in October 1932.

Walshaw Bateman of Skipton (centre) with Imperial Airways Handley Page W 8b *Prince Henry* and living quarters behind. It was quite a rough and ready life touring the country with all these aircraft.

Another Skipton aviation enthusiast was Leslie Smith, who was clerk to the Urban District Council from 1948 to 1969. He knew Earl Fielden and had a flight with him from a field near Barnoldswick. On this occasion the Jubilee Air Display was organised by Owen Cathcart Jones and T. Campbell Black who were leaders in the air race to Australia in October 1934. Pictured, Leslie Smith enjoys a flight with his wife on their honeymoon at Squires Gate.

At Sandylands this parachutist advertises the Co-op.

Nine

At War

Skipton volunteers leave to fight in the First World War. Miss Dyson provided this rare picture which was much in the news in November 1998 – the 80th anniversary of the Armistice.

This First World War camp was alongside Grassington Road near to the Craven Heifer. Many famous regiments such as the Black Watch, The Bantham's and the Bradford Pals passed through here on their way to France.

During the First World War there was a prison camp for Germans situated at the top of Raikes Road. Occasionally artefacts are dug from gardens in Raikeswood Drive. When Mr Fattorini lived at Waysmeet he said that there was a corner post in his garden. One can discover the exact location of the camp from this drawing by a prisoner. The road to Stirton is clearly visible and also the turn off along Sod Hill Lane, now named Raikes Road. Sharphaw can be seen in the distance.

At Christ Church in March 1915 the full military funeral of Tom Clarke took place. He was the eldest son (in a family of sixteen) of Thomas Henry and Pricilla Clarke of 20 Byron Street. A regular soldier in the Green Howards, he was wounded on 11 March 1915 at Neuve Chappelle in France and was brought to Netley Military Hospital in England where he died on 19 March aged twenty-four.

Ada Ann and Will Bruce. Will lost his sight in the First World War and his son Wallace was killed in the Second World War.

After losing his sight Will Bruce was trained as a cobbler by St Dunstan's at one of their Blind Schools. He had a boot and shoe repair shop at Nos 3 and 4 Waller Hill (now the bus station).

Wallace Bruce aged one year and ten months (*above left*) and in uniform (*above right*). Wallace joined the Royal Air Force in November 1941 and trained as an air gunner. In 1943 he joined the crew of Lancaster Bomber ED409 of 106 Squadron Bomber Command based at Syerston, which took off on 31 August 1943 on a mission to Berlin and failed to return. The Lancaster crashed to the north-west of Osnabrück.

Wallace was killed and is buried in Reichwald Forest British Cemetery, Plot 30, Row D, Grave 7. Three crewmembers became prisoners of war.

The officers of the Skipton Home Guard, initially called the Local Defence Volunteers or LDV. Perhaps one factor for the name change was because LDV soon became known by children as 'Look, Duck and Vanish'! Left to right, top: J. Windle, Jack Bramley, J. Cutter, T. Wilman, Dr Annesley Fisher, Ralph Wynn. Middle: Edgar Gunby, Major E. Humphries, Lt. Col. Carruthers, Capt. Bell, Adjutant Fennessay. Front: T. Tyrer.

Ermysted's 1935/36 team. From left to right, top row: Basil Parkman, Hector Capstick, Brook Naylor, Harold Williamson, Arthur Norton, Claude Maxfield, Frank Slater, Alec Nutter, ? Pye, Harry Chester, ? Sunderland. Front row: Jimmy Green, Eddie Kirk, Vincent Tosney (captain), Jack Aldridge. Many of these young men served in the Second World War. One who lost his life was Claude Simpson Maxfield, sixth from left on the top row.

Claude Simpson Maxfield served in the Royal Air Force as a pilot with 104 Squadron. This squadron was sent to serve in Egypt and on 8 September 1942 he was shot down and killed while attacking Tobruk. It was his thirtieth bombing operation. Claude has no known grave. He is remembered by the Runnymede Memorial and in Linton church on a stained glass window.

Claude in Middle East uniform soon after he was rescued after a crash behind enemy lines in the desert.

Sgt. Philip Atha (third from the left) was educated at Brougham Street School and Ermysted's Grammar School where he excelled in sport, particularly cricket, and was captain of the first eleven. He was navigator of Lancaster JB 563 of 100 Squadron which, along with 619 other aircraft, attacked Frankfurt on the night of 22 March 1943. All of the crew were killed except one – a spare navigator who had joined the crew for experience. Philip is buried at Bad Tolz (Dumbach), a British Military Cemetery.

Pilot Officer Stanley Findley was born on 22 May 1915 on Primrose Hill. He was educated at Christ Church School and later worked in car insurance at Cox & Co. He was awarded his 'wings' after training in Canada and then helped to train wireless operators. Eventually, on return to England he became the Captain of a Lancaster LM 522 which, along with 214 others, attacked rocket storage sites north of Paris. Stanley and crew were shot down and killed at Envermeu near Dieppe, where he is buried in the churchyard. The street in the village was named 'Rue Findley 8 Juillet 1944', the date of the crash. He is survived by the daughter he never knew, Lesley Hartley, who is now a physiotherapist at Skipton General Hospital.

Warrant Officer Colin George Dinsdale was born in Skipton on 13 February 1923. He enlisted in the RAF in 1941 after completing his education at Brougham Street and Ermysted's Grammar School. After flying training in the USA he was later posted to Montrose to join a flying instructors course. This did not suit him so after news filtered through that he had flown under the Forth Bridge he was sent off to join 65 Squadron which went to the Second Tactical Air Force in France. He flew Mustangs and was killed in action on 25 July 1944 and is buried at St Hilaire-sur-Pille, France.

Flight Sgt John William Dunford was born in Skipton in 1916. He was educated at Ermysted's Grammar School and then worked at the Craven Electric Company in Keighley Road. Later he was employed as an Engineering Draughtsman with a firm in Tipton, Staffordshire. He was known as 'Jack'. His mother, Celia, was a Skipton woman who opened the Craven Café in Otley Street, which was the first in Skipton. She was the daughter of John William Wilson who had the saddler's shop in Caroline Square, now Dolland's. Jack volunteered for the RAF in 1941 and after training as a navigator he joined a crew posted to 433 Squadron at Skipton-on-Swale in the North Riding. On the night of 22/23 April 1944 his crew took off in Halifax LV 990 on a raid to Dusseldorf and were shot down over the target. The crew are all buried in Reichswald Forest British Military Cemetery. 323 Lanacsters, 254 Halifaxes and 19 Mosquitoes were involved; 29 were shot down.

Sgt Harry Booth, second from the left. After Harry completed his education at the Parish Church School he worked for Ledgard and Wynn but soon joined the RAF and trained as a wireless operator. He was posted to 158 Squadron based at Lissett near Driffield, East Yorkshire. On the night of his death he had joined another Halifax crew to stand in for their regular wireless operator who had been granted home leave to get married; saving his life, as it turned out, at the cost of Harry Booth's. On the night of 23 August 1943 the crew took off in Halifax 4R725 to attack Berlin. The aircraft was shot down and Harry and the second pilot were killed. Pilot Officer A.V. Kyle, the flight engineer, told me that he had not even had time to speak to Harry before or during the operation but he did say that all the crew baled out. Harry is buried in Soltou (Bicklinger) British Military Cemetery.

Sgt John Ashcroft. John lived in Park Avenue and was educated at Ings School and Ermysted's Grammar School. Like his father he trained as a surveyor, working for Skipton Rural District Council at their Granville Street office. He joined the RAF and trained as a navigator in South Africa. Back in England he joined a crew of Wellington HE855 at 26 Operational Training Unit at Wing in Buckinghamshire. On the night of 25 November 1953 he was with a crew of seven who failed to return from cross-country training. They were never found so may have come down in the sea. All the crew's names are on the Runnymede Memorial.

Sgt James Jardine Vaulkhard. James lived in Harewood Road and attended Skipton Girls High School (where they had a kindergarten before the war) and then Ermysted's Grammar School. He was at college in Edinburgh studying medicine when he joined the RAF in 1942 and trained as a navigator. He then joined a Lancaster Pathfinder Squadron No. 156 at Warboys near Huntingdon. They failed to return from a mission to Spezia in Italy on 18 April 1943; they were close to making it back to England, but were shot down at Merville on the coast of France.

Sgt Jack Archer. Another old boy of Ermysted's Grammar School who served in the RAF as a wireless operator and air gunner. He joined the crew of Hampden AE 247 of 61 Squadron based at North Luffenham and was shot down and killed on a mission to Frankfurt on 29 August 1941. Jack had actually been due to go on leave and planned to join his parents on holiday in Blackpool to celebrate his twenty-first birthday. This was cancelled when another crewmember went sick and Jack had to take his place. His aunt, Mrs Foster who had Wendy's Café in Skipton, took the telegram to Blackpool. Jack's sister, Mrs Barron of Carleton, who was with her parents, remembers it as though it were only yesterday.

Lt. Thomas Fattorini, Royal Flying Corps, second son of Mrs T. Fattorini 'Rockwood' Skipton. He was lost in action on 13 August 1918 while flying over enemy lines on a voluntary photographic reconnaissance flight. He was nineteen. This photograph is in the book *Craven's Part in the Great War*. The book was compiled and edited by John T. Clayton, editor of the *Craven Herald*, assisted by Thos Brayshaw JP. Walter Morrison JP of Maltham Tarn generously defrayed the whole cost of the publication and it was presented to each member of His Majesty's Forces who joined up from the Skipton Parliamentary Division, or to their next of kin.